CUTTING TEETH

Cutting
Teeth

Jesse Holwitz

San Francisco, California

ISBN-13: 978-1-7374947-4-4

Cover artwork by Bruce McGaw

Author photo by Juliette Colas

San Francisco, California

CONTENTS

PREFACE: THE GENESIS OF SOME NEW QUESTION

Of all the arts, poetry is perhaps the most intimate. Confessional poetry intensifies this exposure. The poet lays bare his, her or their human experience in the intimate space of the page. Even when the poet adopts the tools of social buffering – e.g. bravado, misdirection, humor or wry dispassion – there is a raw nakedness to the sensation of holding someone's most necessary confessions (quite literally in book form) in the palm of one's hands.

In his debut collection, Jesse Holwitz manages to stand at the center of his verse without employing any evident social scaffolding. His is not the cry of a latter-day Beat confessor, but an honest, convincing, and thus refreshingly penetrating and bold new voice. *Cutting Teeth* reminds us how powerfully we can be affected by the invitation to feel what another feels.

These poems are shadowy and elusive though self-aware. Holwitz claims our attention in the opening line of the first poem, "Prologue" with the lines: "I have never lived dick to dick." The reader's mind may be drawn to the obvious places, but none would anticipate the arresting emotional backdrop of "nine-eleven" or the searing intensity of the final image. One somehow understands from this very initial poem that this is a poet who would never detonate language merely for effect. He is too serious in the best sense of the word to play tricks or rely on shock-value. He is taking us down to our knees so that we may be moved in ways that matter.

What follow are more distillations of a human experience. None extend longer than a page. *Cutting Teeth,* the title of the collection, reminds us that this is a young poet working his craft – i.e. learning by doing. But there is also a sharp and quick bite to these poems. There is no needless working of the jaw or chewing overly-long on ideas or images. Holwitz doesn't fall prey to the guilty pleasure of rolling words around on the tongue to show off his deft facility with language. I've not read poetry in a long while that made me contemplate and challenge my balance of self-indulgence versus forthrightness.

There is a line from the poem "Grief" that it strikes me speaks to Holwitz's poetic process: "the breaking and mending of yesterday." Here is another from "Ode": "undress your freshest wound and let me/become a surgeon." And from "Wheatfield Hunger": "turn my body toward its winter." We arrive in "20" at:

and now I'm open
hollow like glass
that tries to warn you
by cutting teeth

The collection ends with a poem called "Dawn." The decision to end the collection on a horizon resonates. The reader almost feels the effect of morning light. I, for one, look forward to what comes next.

Tamsin Spencer Smith
San Francisco, CA

PROLOGUE

I've never lived dick to dick.
I've never let my knees get red hot in neon moonlight.
But I'm sure that Nathan felt the emotional fallout of nine-eleven
in his tonsils.

I've never seen Nathan try as hard as he did that day.
I've never tried that hard.
He just walked into the gray cloud of soot
He just went in there
Without a mask.
He made his way through rubble
He made his way through red rubble
Without any real direction.
He fucking cried his eyes out and he kept wiping his nose
And he fucking cried his eyes out
And Nathan gave the best blowjob of his life buried in the red
rubble.

REMEMBERING

my pockets filled up with
mud or when every other streetlamp lost
power it was disorienting more
than anything else
and I hope,
at least, that
it's what made you such a restless sleeper the next morning
I tried as hard as I
could to eat cereal
without looking at your
chest you
said you were *going on a walk with emily later*
today and now
it's impossible to
remember anything that wasn't
naming or
planning or
hauling you up the
stairs at night and
especially the smell of a limp body when it's
nearly dropped months
later when I stop in front of your door
to light a fire like mothers
do when they
sleepwalk I promise that it's just action for action's sake
like blind rhythm or
flailing your arms until
your fingers ache and that I was cold
when it happened.

RESTLESSNESS

Maybe it's the deprivation of oxygen that makes a cigarette so
delectable in the
morning, manipulating the spirit of breath to get something better,
an alchemy of the lungs,
being in chorus with something besides air, wrapping the mystery
of it between my fingertips, in and out, the key and the door,
retreating back into my room, where the light of infinity haunts my
ceiling, casting new shadows and patterns across blank slates, the
genesis of some new question, the impending reality of some new
answer, fear of truth and its vigilant warden who wrestles with the
circumference of knowledge, who shapes imagination into perfect
little
circles, who patrols the sacred boundary between what is known
and what cannot be
known, who is without shape or form, who manifests in the
hunger of a mountain lion, the look that people give
when they are too distraught to speak, death in the
room.

Maybe god is on tenterhooks, as tense as my
back becomes lying in bed so long.

FOR ME, AT LEAST

He doesn't search for the fish anymore
content to let them swim through the back of his mind
not hungry for their flesh
just patient for the bear and
the heron
who discuss him over dinner
He is a *broken* man
says the heron
He will *ruin* us
says the bear
and now my father's feet are cold in the water
so I will take him beneath a warm quilt
it's not his time yet
for me, at least.

ONLY HUMAN

Born a mailman, delivering daisy chains and
blossoms in time for spring, delivering plastic
ledgers filled with blood, delivering love birds and
terrapins, leaving notes, leaving the station step by
step, leaving each day as parcel on the doorstep of
the next, and today I've decided to open your letter
again, to read each word in your voice, and
no, I am not a mailman, I am not yours anymore, I am
not silver, none of this is true — I'm only human, beneath
scorching memory, only human, delivering myself the bad
news of what we had, delivering myself from abandon, leaving
metaphor and simile, leaving all the figurative elements of your
body,
replacing them with madness, replacing them with the helplessly
abstract, meeting patrons of despair, meeting emptiness in
dawnlight, meeting myself in the mirror, and no, I am not a
mailman, not a forgotten hair on your pillow, not an
inkblot in your day, not a fragment of speech in your mouth.

GRIEF

The breaking and mending of yesterday
limps up to my door, a pool-cue in his
left hand, a badger in his right —
I rack up the arbiters, whisper the
prayer — the game isn't a metaphor for anything — it's just
tuesday
saying goodbye to monday, the erasure of pain, sinners counting
spades — it's simple.

And once it's all over, the breaking and
mending of yesterday puts out his cigarette,
leans in close — badger on his breath — and
croaks:

> the truth was somewhere
> a long time ago.

SHE'S RIGHT ABOUT ME

I am a plastic machine
with a silver spoon that goes in and out of my little mouth over and
over again
my automaton body relaxed because the movement of my arm
feels real
the spoon helping me think that I am bigger than myself
powered in full by inward thoughts of prophethood
but I am not divine,
and she knows that it hurts me

2021 GHAZAL

Take your human-home and make a funeral pyre – rejoice
in echo, shadow – rejoice in the letting go of it all.

Algorithms have outpaced the feeling of your hand in my
hand – digital fingers prod the tongues of my family to dust.

When will the hermits peel back their skin, when will the jesters
kneel, when will the moneylenders get naked in the sun?

Yesterday was just bayonets courting the favor of masterpiece,
today
we walk in circles around the bloodshed – ants rubbernecking from
the hivemind.

The night still comes – fog rolls, knuckles whitten, in-breath and
out-breath, paths dissolve in the snow – it all ends in the end.

—

12/17/21

You know where I am today – between the
        skin and the spirit, beneath a waterfall, scrawling
                blueprints in the sand, handing myself to invisible
anniversaries.

Each name has a shadow – filled to the brim with mountains,
        filled to the brim with nectar – a whispering fingertrap, a
collection
                of decaying philosophy.

Your shadow shoots across my feet and I feel the weight of
        God's left index finger on my spine – your name is the
drowning, your name
                is the bear

        and

you know where I am today – between the haunt and
        the seance, beneath a hill, praying for Land's End to
                become a funeral pyre, praying for the sound of a
horn.

SONG

Climb that second birth and light a candle
at the top – let wax coat the pillar of
history beneath your feet – disdaining it – breathe
heavy – breathe like you're about to jump
a chasm – like you've just escaped hell –
take your first steps and call yourself a
man – curled fists and strung calves – hear
the heart beating as one – smell the afterbirth on
your breath – become something real – become
nicotine – become wood – the candle burns
and life is a blooming orchid – the candle burns and
the world begins.

20

I was the mirror
I was the shelter
of kinship gathered
and money spent

and once I emptied
my burden cup
first for my sake
then for the gun

I took my life
into my hands
and I took the sap
from a hungry pine

fused them hot
beneath my palm
until the holy deed
was done

and now I'm open
hollow like glass
that tries to warn you
by cutting teeth

and saying "no"
and promising when
a date is set
to re-burn the sand

ODE

It feels so good
when you bring me silver door knobs and dandelion
stems. It feels so good when you look at my body like a furnace.

Pull my hair and watch me rearrange the pain as if it were a puzzle.
Take me home and
migraine yourself into myself.

You and I were travelers, somewhere in
Germany, twelve dollars to the man with the top hat and he
danced for us – what kind of dream is this now?

Take away your golden buttons and pearled
tin – undress your freshest wound and let me
become a surgeon. You and I were in the garden
once, and it felt so good to melt our flesh and fuse
into the shape of a lonely and tired man –
I stared at you as if you were the sun.

THE SKY FALLS OUT

Because I'm a plank of wood
Because my life used to be pristine
Because I'm developing a stutter
Because the moon throws up all night
Because everyone has to practice death
Because my feet are calloused
Because I'm lost in the forest
Because we're underwater again
Because my head is heavy
Because you left me at the altar
Because the mountains whisper hymns
Because there's a blood diamond in my chest
Because you're still gone
Because the past is leather
Because I broke

SPRINTER FROM THE STANDS

Something about her
disposition hunkers in
the back of my mind like
a wounded soldier, and I say
peace, but
she says
faster, lesser,
subtraction,
weightlessness.

From so far away she is a shouting
quasar, a weekend bender – the sound
of steel against steel.

Up close she dies so gracefully –
running in circles, just running in
circles.

WHEATFIELD HUNGER

Wheatfield hunger like a jack in the dealer's hand
Nobody told me the weight of the world rests on the tips of our
fingers
Machination sick and tired of the endless plan

So sick and tired that I let my body forget to stand
Everybody blue and weeping until the feeling forgets to linger
Wheatfield hunger like a jack in the dealer's hand

Death comes washing over my shoulder from the sigh of an
oscillating fan
Nobody is weeping, nobody cash now, nobody paper, nobody
linger
Machination sick and tired of the endless plan

Watch me hunger one more time like a dying sycophant
Burning fuel for the change in my pocket to sting a hole in my
pants like ginger
Wheatfield hunger like a jack in the dealer's hand

Turn away from my body like a crow turning away from the land
Help me help myself – turn my body toward its winter
Machination sick and tired of the endless plan

Lost without a means to understand
Lost and as dead as cinder
Wheatfield hunger like a jack in the dealer's hand
Machination sick and tired of the endless plan

EMPTY

I
don't have a
job sometimes when I arch my
back over and
around the bend of a wooden
railing I can really feel
what it's like to have a
spine and tendrils working
together every single time I
take a shower I swear to god
I know what it's like I swear
to god every time I
even look at a large body of
water it's human
but why
did it feel so flat
to walk the trees like dogs and I
really mean that, I mean
that I walked them like
they were *dogs*
last summer
and I still don't understand it that's
 what I really mean it's
the thing that you said to
me *I want it to stop being a thing that I think about*
I still don't understand it we
had a baby once and
maybe it's just supposed to
get worse.

FIRE

There is fire
everywhere, on the uneasy
sunlight shooting between tree-branch
shadows –
on the rims of a sugar cube.

Fire seeps into my periphery –
waking up
in hospital beds, or
watching my father slowly dismember a tissue,
crying, and

          I have spent entire years praising water, the
    melatonin on
my desk, the hanging portrait of you next to my bed, but all of that
means
nothing now – novelty scorches the earth, my life ablaze,
everything red.

IN THE MIRROR BENEATH PUFFER'S POND

turning into myself
and weeping
beneath our features of
starving and eyebrows and fungus
that smile "hello" and "good
morning" and "tu
esday" an
d "rutabaga"
and "rutabaga"

EULOGY

Sometimes you have to walk alone, facing time and hunting for solace
in dark nights – paving the way toward novel sunsets and daydreams.

Sometimes you have to lose everything just to find a mirror in the core of an apple,
and sometimes the mirror has no words for the future – sometimes there's only lamentation:

> Hug me one more time, hold
> my body, I've forgotten the smell of your hair.

DAWN

It's the molten core of the earth holding my body, heating the wax off my
shoulders, slowly putting me to sleep, illuminating the ocean blue mobile that hangs above my head.

In a dream, my father asks me:

>   Have you seen the woman
>   stuck to the sun? I strain my eyes against the
>   morning light.

Jesse Holwitz, 2019

Jesse Holwitz was born and raised in San Francisco, where he still resides. After studying at Hampshire College in Amherst MA, he developed a strong passion for poetry. This is his first collection. In 2021, Jesse was diagnosed with bipolar-depression; he hopes to channel the voice of the many who struggle with this condition in his work. In his free time, Jesse enjoys playing chess and taking long walks in the woods.

THE PAGE POETS SERIES

Number 1
Between First & Second Sleep by Tamsin Spencer Smith

Number 2
The Michaux Notebook by Micah Ballard

Number 3
Sketch of the Artist by Patrick James Dunagan

Number 4
Different Darknesses by Jason Morris

Number 5
Suspension of Mirrors by Mary Julia Klimenko

Number 6
The Rise & Fall of Johnny Volume by Garrett Caples

Number 7
Used with Permission by Charlie Pendergast

Number 8
Deconfliction by Katharine Harer

Number 9
Unlikely Saviors by Stan Stone

Number 10
Beauty Will Be Convulsive by Matt Gonzalez

Number 11
Displacement Geology by Tamsin Spencer Smith

Number 12
The Public Sound by Marina Lazzara

Number 13
Record of Records by Rod Roland

Number 14
Strangers We Have Known by John Briscoe

Number 15
Cutting Teeth by Jesse Holwitz